Unlocking The Secrets Of Expecting Mothers:

Your Complete Guide to a Healthy, Happy Nine Months

Evelyn T. Whitley

Table of Content

Chapter 1:
Are You pregnant?

Pregnancy happens when a sperm fertilizes an egg after it's released from the ovary during ovulation. The fertilized egg then travels down into the uterus, where implantation happens. A successful implantation results in pregnancy.

On average, a full-term pregnancy lasts 40 weeks. Several elements might affect a pregnancy. Women who obtain an early pregnancy diagnosis and prenatal care are more likely to enjoy a healthy pregnancy and give birth to a healthy baby.

Knowing what to anticipate throughout the complete pregnant term is vital for monitoring both your health and the health of the baby. If you'd prefer to avoid conception, there are additional effective kinds of birth control you should keep in mind.

Symptoms of Pregnancy

You may notice certain signs and symptoms before you ever take a pregnancy test. Others may show weeks later, as your hormone levels alter.

Missed period

Missing menstruation is one of the early signs of pregnancy (and maybe the most typical one) (and maybe the most classic one). However, a missing period doesn't always imply you're pregnant, particularly if your cycle tends to be erratic.

There are several health issues other than pregnancy that might cause late or missing menstruation.

Headache

Headaches are typical in early pregnancy. They're frequently caused by changing hormone levels and increased blood volume. Contact your doctor if your headaches don't go away or are very severe.

Spotting

Some women may have minor bleeding and spotting in early pregnancy. This bleeding is most typically the outcome of implantation. Implantation normally happens one to two weeks following conception.

Early pregnancy bleeding may also develop from very modest issues such as an infection or discomfort. The latter typically affects the surface of the cervix (which is especially sensitive during pregnancy) (which is very sensitive during pregnancy).

Bleeding may occasionally suggest a major pregnancy issue, such as miscarriage, ectopic pregnancy, or placenta previa. Always contact your doctor if you're worried.

Weight gain

You should anticipate gaining between 1 and 4 pounds in your first few months of pregnancy. Weight gain becomes more evident at the beginning of your second trimester.

Pregnancy-induced hypertension

High blood pressure, or hypertension, sometimes occurs during pregnancy. A lot of variables may raise your risk, including \ being overweight or obese \ and smoking

When having a history or having a family history of pregnancy-induced hypertension

Heartburn

Hormones generated during pregnancy may occasionally loosen the valve between your stomach and esophagus. When stomach acid spills out, this might result in heartburn.

Constipation

Hormone changes during early pregnancy might slow down your digestive system. As a consequence, you may get constipated.

Cramps

As the muscles in your uterus begin to stretch and develop, you may experience a tugging feeling that mimics menstruation pains. If spotting or blood occurs with your cramps, it might signify a miscarriage or an ectopic pregnancy.

Back pain

Hormones and tension in the muscles are the primary causes of back discomfort in early pregnancy. Later on, your increased weight and shifting center of gravity may contribute to your back discomfort. Around half of all pregnant women feel back discomfort throughout their pregnancy.

Anemia

Pregnant women have an increased risk of anemia, which produces symptoms such as lightheadedness and dizziness.

The syndrome may lead to preterm delivery and low birth weight. Prenatal care frequently includes screening for anemia.

Depression

Between 14 and 23 percent of all pregnant women suffer depression throughout their pregnancy. The various bodily and mental changes you undergo might be significant reasons.

Be careful to notify your doctor if you don’t feel like your regular self.

Insomnia

Insomnia is another typical symptom of early pregnancy. Stress, physical pain, and hormonal fluctuations all be contributory reasons. A balanced diet, excellent sleep habits, and yoga stretches may all help you obtain a good night's sleep.

Breast changes

Breast changes are one of the earliest apparent indications of pregnancy. Even before you're far enough along for a positive test, your breasts may begin to feel sensitive, swollen, and generally heavy or full. Your nipples may also get bigger and more sensitive, and the areolae may darken.

Acne

Because of elevated androgen hormones, many women have acne in early pregnancy. These hormones may make your face oilier, which can block pores. Pregnancy acne is generally transient and clears up once the baby is delivered.

Vomiting

This is a component of “morning sickness,” a frequent symptom that normally starts during the first four months. Morning sickness is frequently the first indicator that you’re pregnant. Increased hormones during early pregnancy are the major culprit.

Hip discomfort

This is prevalent throughout pregnancy and tends to intensify in late pregnancy. It might have a multitude of reasons, including \spressure on your ligaments.

Diarrhea and other stomach issues occur often during pregnancy. Hormone changes, a changing diet, and additional stress are all plausible factors. If diarrhea lasts longer than a few days, call your doctor to make sure you don't get dehydrated.

Stress and pregnancy

While pregnancy is normally a pleasant time, it may sometimes be a source of stress. A new baby brings enormous changes to your body, your connections, and even your money. Don't hesitate to approach your doctor for support if you begin to feel overwhelmed.

The bottom line

If you suspect you may be pregnant, you shouldn't depend exclusively on these signs and symptoms for proof. Taking a home pregnancy test or contacting your doctor for lab testing may confirm a probable pregnancy.

Many of these signs and symptoms might also be caused by other health issues, such as premenstrual syndrome (PMS) (PMS).

Chapter 2: Pregnancy secrets you didn't know about

The problem is that no one discusses these pregnant secrets. We either forget (or have selective recall!) about what it was like, or we presume people won't care to know what we went through. Other issues might be too delicate to speak about, depending on whom you talk to.

Well, I'd want to be the person to tell you what I wish I knew about the pregnancy. Below are my top 11 pregnancy secrets no one tells you about

1. You can't sleep on your back

I'm the sort who tosses throughout the night, trying to find that comfortable position to go back to sleep. And the position I enjoy the most is sleeping on my back.

Turns out that after a few months of being pregnant, we can't sleep on our backs anymore. The weight of the baby and the placenta press down too heavily, leading us to wake up short of breath and worried.

Instead, the optimum sleeping posture is to lie on your left side, which is the greatest method to send blood and oxygen to the baby and placenta.

I thought sleep deprivation only happened after the baby is delivered. While disturbed sleep isn't the same as waking up to a screaming infant, I was nevertheless astonished to hear sleep troubles begin long before the kid even arrived.

2. You pee a lot

This is one of the adverse effects of pregnancy that practically every pregnant woman suffers. Throughout your pregnancy, particularly in the third trimester, you'll use the bathroom—I'm not kidding—about an hour every day.

We're already so enormous at that stage that waddling to the restroom is no easy effort, even for the healthiest of pregnant women. But since the kid is by then so enormous, our bladders are forced down and can't store the same quantity as another lady not having a baby.

Plus, pregnant women are instructed to consume plenty of water to minimize possible early contractions and edema. Drinking additional water without the bladder's ability to manage it explains why pregnant women urinate frequently.

3. Your hands and feet will swell

Before having kids, I saw pregnant women as expanding in size solely in the abdominal region. After all, that's where the baby develops, not somewhere else. So, imagine my astonishment when I realized we also swell in other regions of our body, notably our hands and feet.

Not everyone swells, and each pregnancy is different. When I was pregnant with the twins, my fingers were so huge I removed my wedding bands for fear they'd get trapped (I wore them on a choker chain instead) (I wore them on a necklace chain instead). And my feet became so huge I couldn't wear closed-toe shoes anymore.

If your body expands, drink lots of water and put your feet higher than your heart. For instance, lay on your side on the sofa and put your feet on the armrest.

4. Morning sickness is no joke

I had visualized the traditional pregnant lady bent over a toilet seat but didn't understand much about morning sickness. For anybody who has ever felt hung over after a crazy night of alcohol, that's pretty much what it's like, but every day.

You have no appetite (previously beloved meals are now disgusting), feel dizzy with little movements, and have the want to vomit up all the time, even though you never do. And I'm not sure who came up with the "morning" portion of morning sickness, but we're talking the entire day, too.

Imagine feeling that way, every day, for many weeks (and for some unlucky few, their whole pregnancy) (and for some unfortunate few, their entire pregnancy). That's morning sickness.

5. You're just consuming an additional 300 calories

I'm sure the expression "eating for two" meant dining for two people, but not two persons of the same size. I figured pregnant women needed to eat a lot given how much we expand, but it turns out, we just require an additional 300 calories each day.

Lactating women require more calories (an additional 500) than pregnant ones.

If you want a visual of what 300 calories looks like, think a bowl of cereal with milk, or a baked potato—not exactly a buffet feast.

Pregnant women need to gain weight by eating nutritious food in a moderate and progressive method, not by binging on junk food with thousands of calories aplenty.

6. Your hair and nails will look wonderful

We don't have many rewards and pleasures from being pregnant, but one of them is having gorgeous hair and nails. Prenatal vitamins include additional calcium for your baby's development that also finds its way to your hair and nails.

Another cosmetic bonus of being pregnant is you'll have bigger breasts, too. Your body will develop milk glands and prepare itself to breastfeed your kid. Then after the baby is delivered, your breasts will swell even more as it anticipates producing the milk (for a total of two size increases for me!).

7. You'll feel pelvic discomfort after your pregnancy

I had coasted along quite nicely with my first pregnancy, but around the eight-month point, my bones started feeling squeezed. It seemed as though a giant rock was attempting to pound my pelvic bones from above.

No wonder pregnant women waddle, particularly during that final month. The weight of the baby and all your body fluids are pressing down, forcing you to experience the agony that you may have been able to escape for most of your pregnancy.

This is the time to lay down as much as possible, alleviating the weight of your pelvis and transferring it to the rest of your body.

8. You probably won't go to the hospital immediately soon

I blame the media and movies for the misleading images of a pregnant lady running to the hospital the minute she feels a contraction. Not true!

You'll start your labor at home and will remain for many hours before traveling to the hospital, particularly if this is your first pregnancy. (Labor with subsequent pregnancies likely to progress faster than your first.)

I'd heard of rapid labor, the sort when you're hurried to the hospital because the baby is coming any minute now, but such are unusual. You'll likely instead have plenty of time to labor at home, even sleep, pack last-minute things, and have a light lunch.

9. Your body might tremor during delivery

It occurred in both of my pregnancies: Right as I was pushing and delivering, my body started to tremble like crazy. My teeth were chattering as though I had walked outdoors in deep snow wearing just a t-shirt and shorts.

At first, I felt I was scared, but my doctor told me the trembling was normal and was my body's way of dealing with the fluctuations in hormones.

10. You deliver more than just the baby

While the baby is in your womb, the placenta becomes its source of food and oxygen. Before kids, I never even realized pregnant women were also carrying a placenta, much less that we'd also deliver it once the baby is born.

But don't worry—the placenta is nothing like delivering the baby. It doesn't take rigorous pushing to come out, particularly because it's a blob and your kid has already prepared the road.

11. You'll appear like you're six months pregnant after giving birth

Even after delivering the baby and the placenta, your body won't shrink back to its pre-baby size straight soon. Instead, you'll walk home looking like you did when you were six months pregnant. (Keep this in mind as you consider what to pack or wear those first few weeks following giving birth.)

Your uterus does shrink quite rapidly compared to how long it took to develop, but it surely won't be instantaneous or even overnight. It'll likely go back to its pre-baby size four to six weeks after giving delivery.

Still, it's important to be prepared and know what to anticipate or what could happen. And that, despite my first preconceptions, pregnancy is much more than labor and giving birth, but the nine months before it.

Chapter 3: 21 Top Guides for Expecting Mothers

Pregnant women are filled with both optimism and fear. Will my child be okay? Will I? Moms-to-be is also looking for ways to help them enjoy their pregnancy and deal with the inevitable issues. Where better to seek advice than from mothers who are also medical doctors?

1. **Managing Cravings**

During pregnancy, many women have intense food cravings for certain meals. You've surely heard stories of loved ones being despatched at odd hours to get a specific brand of bacon double cheeseburger or rocky road ice cream to satisfy a pregnant mother's need. Perhaps you've experienced an intense need to spend personally.

Nobody knows why some pregnant women experience food cravings. "Some experts say cravings, and their opposite, food aversions, are protective," says Siobhan Dolan, MD, assistant medical director of the March of Dimes Birth Defects Foundation and assistant professor of obstetrics and gynecology and women's health at Albert Einstein College of Medicine in New York.

For example, you may not want to consume alcohol when pregnant, which is advantageous since avoiding beer, wine, and other spirits promotes your baby's mental and physical development.

Others believe that a pregnant woman's love for salty potato chips is nature's way of helping her reach her daily sodium limit. However, it is exceedingly improbable that cells convert nutritional deficiencies into food demands. Longing for a specific dish distinguishes pregnancy food cravings from desires women experience when they are not pregnant.

Pregnancy Cravings Are in a League of Their Own

So your food cravings are most likely a result of pregnancy hormones. Hormonal changes during pregnancy heighten the sense of smell (which greatly impacts taste) and have the potential to influence dietary choices.

"Women who are feeling queasy, bloated, exhausted, or grumpy as a result of the impacts of pregnancy hormones may seek meals to boost their comfort level," explains Elisa Zied, a registered dietitian and American Dietetic Association representative. "Some women who starve themselves when they aren't pregnant see pregnancy as an opportunity to indulge in things they normally shun."

Zied chose meals she enjoyed as a teen but ate significantly less often in the years before her two pregnancies. During her first pregnancy, Zied craved kielbasa and melted cheese on toasted English muffins. She favored Cheez-Its above anything else when she was expecting her second kid.

How does a nutritionist who knows the better deal with cravings? By consuming tiny amounts of lower-fat versions of one's favorite meals. "When I wanted certain things, I wanted them," she adds, "so I gave in, always cognizant of how much I was consuming."

Food Cravings Aren't Always Negative

The meals that women like are, in fact, healthy options. Dairy products, for example, are high in protein, calcium, and other minerals and are among the top foods desired by pregnant women, according to the March of Dimes. When Dolan was pregnant, all she wanted to drink was cranberry juice. Fortified cranberry juice is a wonderful source of calcium and vitamin C, as well as a variety of other minerals required during pregnancy.

Food cravings might vary from pregnancy to pregnancy. They may also alter from one day to the next. Don't be shocked if the stuff you had to eat yesterday makes you gag today. Pregnancy may permanently alter one's eating choices. Dolan's passion for cranberry juice faded after giving birth. "I won't even go near it anymore," she adds.

Pica is a syndrome in which some women develop a need for nonfood objects such as ice, dirt, clay, paper, and even paint chips. Pica may indicate an iron deficit. Expectant moms may also feel compelled to consume flour or cornstarch, which, although constituting food, may be harmful in high quantities. Too much may cause constipation and drown out the nutrients your baby needs by making you feel full. If you develop any of these cravings, prevent consuming them and notify your doctor immediately away.

Regardless of how strong your desire is, avoid foods that are considered health concerns for pregnant women and growing newborns. These are some examples:

- Seafood, meat, and eggs, both raw and undercooked
- Unpasteurized milk and its derivatives, such as Brie, feta, Camembert, Roquefort, and Mexican-style cheeses
- Juice unpasteurized
- Alfalfa, clover, and radish sprouts are examples of raw vegetable sprouts.
- Teas made from herbs
- Alcohol

It is possible to experience food cravings while still providing your kid with the nutrition he or she needs to thrive. However, giving in to your craving for high-calorie meals too often may result in excessive weight gain. Excessive weight gain raises the risk of gestational diabetes and high blood pressure.

Here's how to deal with cravings throughout pregnancy:

- Consume a well-balanced diet that includes lean protein sources, low-fat dairy products, whole grains, fruits, vegetables, and legumes. A tiny piece of a less-than-healthy item will not drown out the nourishment your baby need if your diet is balanced.

- Eat frequently to prevent blood sugar decreases, which may lead to food cravings. Food may be divided into six modest and fulfilling meals.
- Incorporate frequent physical exercise (as permitted by your doctor).
- If the want to eat brownie sundaes has taken over your life, try distracting yourself by going for a brief walk; going on an errand (but avoid the grocery store!); getting out of the kitchen; contacting a friend; or reading.
- Instead of the king-size, satiate your sweet need with a bar of fun-size chocolate. Do you have to have chips? To decrease fat intake and total consumption, use a snack-size bag of baked chips.
- Choose low-calorie foods. When you want super-premium ice cream, frozen yogurt

and low-fat fudge bars may suffice. Other low-calorie frozen sweets that may be substituted for higher-calorie alternatives include sorbet, sherbet, and frozen fruit bars.

- Make more healthy substitutes for the delights you desire. If you must have a strawberry Danish, put two teaspoons of whipped cream cheese on four graham cracker pieces. Serve with strawberry preserves or fresh strawberries. Another option: Instead of buying a milkshake, try this blender treat: combine low-fat vanilla frozen yogurt and orange juice and whip until desired consistency is reached.

Cravings are typical throughout pregnancy and do not indicate that anything is wrong. If you have a yearning for anything unhealthy, consider eating something healthy instead, such as yogurt instead of ice cream.

But if you really must have that ice cream, go ahead and consume it. Dr. Erika Schwartz, is a mother of two and a women's health expert in New York City.

2. Swelling Relief

Swelling is typical during pregnancy, especially in the legs, ankles, feet, and fingers.

It's usually worst towards the end of the day and later in the pregnancy.

Swelling that develops gradually is normally not dangerous to you or your baby, although it may be unpleasant.

A rapid rise in swelling may be an indication of pre-eclampsia, which should be treated as soon as possible.

- swelling in your face, hands, or feet that appear suddenly
- a severe headache

- visual issues, such as blurring or flashing lights in your eyes
- terrible discomfort under your ribcage

If you have any of these symptoms, you should avoid vomiting.

These might be pre-eclampsia symptoms, which can lead to major consequences if not watched and addressed.

Swelling is normal throughout pregnancy.

When you're pregnant, your body holds more water than normal, which causes swelling.

Extra water tends to collect in the lowest regions of the body during the day, particularly if the weather is hot or you have been standing a lot.

Blood flow in your legs might be affected by the pressure of your developing womb. This might result in fluid accumulation in your legs, ankles, and feet.

What may assist with swelling?

Try to:

- Avoid standing for lengthy periods of time.
- Wear comfortable shoes and socks, and avoid anything with tight straps or that might pinch your feet if they swell.
- Try to relax as much as possible with your feet elevated.
- Drink lots of water - this will assist your body in getting rid of extra water.
- Exercise - Try to go for daily walks or conduct foot exercises.

Exercises for the feet

You can perform foot exercises while sitting or standing. They improve blood circulation, reduce ankle swelling, and prevent calf muscle cramps:

- 30 times, bend and extend your foot up and down.
- Each foot should be rotated in a circle 8 times in one direction and 8 times the other.

“My feet and fingers swelled during pregnancy. I used to put my feet up whenever I could, particularly at night when watching TV. It's a good idea to have a footstool handy.

It also helps to remain hydrated, which may seem counterintuitive. If you're swollen, don't stop drinking. I drank a lot of water and the odd caffeinated beverage. Dr. Aline Tanios, a pediatrician and hospitalist at Arkansas Children's Hospital in Little Rock, is a mother of three."

3. Managing Morning Sickness

I had severe morning sickness throughout my first pregnancy. But I discovered one really efficient remedy: raw ginger.

I finely diced a thumbnail-size piece of fresh ginger root and soaked it in boiling water for two to three minutes, much like tea. I could drink it all day and chew on the ginger at the bottom of each cup. My nausea was reduced by roughly half. Nothing else, not even prescription medicines, worked as well. Dr. Ann Kulze is a mother of four and the author of "Dr. Ann's 10-Step Diet: A Simple Plan for Permanent Weight Loss and Lifelong Vitality."

Morning sickness remedies include:

- Stay away from your dislikes.

This may seem to be a no-brainer but bear with us. If the scent or taste of food that you normally love makes you sick, don't force yourself to consume it. This applies to food you believe you should be consuming (ask your doctor about alternatives) as well as food prepared by others, even with the greatest of intentions. Tracking your symptoms might help you pinpoint your triggers!

- Small, high-carbohydrate meals are ideal.

Avoid big meals and foods heavy in sugar or fat. Small servings of bland, carbohydrate-rich items such as rice, bananas, and bread will be easy on your stomach. Snack on them throughout the day to prevent feeling hungry; an empty stomach may cause nausea!

- Ginger has become your new best buddy.

Ginger has been shown to alleviate nausea and vomiting. Sipping ginger tea while keeping hydrated is a fantastic strategy to decrease nausea. Ginger supplements are another excellent choice, but consult your doctor or pharmacist before including them in your diet.

- Consume lots of water.

When you're suffering from morning sickness, keeping hydrated is critical. Keep a water bottle nearby and drink tiny, regular sips. Drinking in this manner will keep you hydrated and prevent you from feeling nauseous from taking huge gulps. If the flavor of plain water isn't tempting, make your own infused water by adding ice cubes, mint leaves, lemon, or raspberries.

- Before getting out of bed, eat something simple.

To prevent that empty-stomach feeling, eat something dry before getting out of bed in the morning. Place some crackers on your nightstand before going to bed, or have your spouse bring you a piece of toast before you get out of bed. There has never been a greater reason to have breakfast in bed!

- Put your zzz's first.

Being ill may make you weary, and being fatigued can exacerbate nausea. What a terrible circle! Take brief naps throughout the day to overcome weariness. This will assist to alleviate nausea and allow your body some well-deserved rest.

- Attempt alternative therapy.

Morning sickness may occasionally be relieved with aromatherapy, acupressure, and hypnosis. Even if alternative remedies aren't normally your thing, sometimes they're necessary! Consult your doctor about which treatments are safe to use throughout pregnancy, and then relax.

- What to keep an eye out for

Morning sickness is painful but not dangerous for the majority of expectant mothers. Some women, however, may endure extreme nausea and vomiting, preventing them from consuming any food or drinks. This is known as hyperemesis gravidarum (HG), and it often necessitates hospitalization to prevent dehydration. If you are having any of the following symptoms, please contact your healthcare provider:

- You are unable to keep any beverages down.
- You feel very tired or dizzy.
- You're not urinating.
- Your heart is pounding.

If severe nausea is affecting your daily life, arrange an appointment with your doctor as soon as possible. They will take you through how to manage your symptoms and assess if you need more medication.

The main point

Morning sickness may be difficult to deal with in the first few months of pregnancy, but perhaps these ideas will help you find relief.

The good news is that nausea normally goes away during the second trimester, allowing you to concentrate on your developing baby and look forward to seeing him or her!

4. Observing Strange Tastes and Smells

What can I do if I have a heightened sense of smell when pregnant?

You can't chop your nose off, but you may attempt to avoid odors that irritate you (especially those that ramp up your nausea and other pregnancy symptoms). Attempt the following strategies:

- Eat wisely. Cook and eat only foods that you can tolerate the smell of. Even if you liked cauliflower and broccoli when you were younger, you might not like the smell of cooked cruciferous vegetables when you're pregnant.
- Clean up. To eliminate cooking or musty scents, keep your windows open whenever feasible.
- Maintain cleanliness. Wash your garments more often than normal since fibers tend to retain scents.

- Baby your nose. Saline washes and sprays may help keep your nasal passages wet and healthy (and also assist with congestion, another typical pregnant problem) (and also help with congestion, another common pregnancy complaint).
- Ditch deodorants. Change to unscented or mildly scented toiletries and cleaning products (or ones with smells that do not make you ill).
- Request special attention. Inquire with your spouse, family, friends, and adjacent colleagues whether they can detect your newly enhanced sense of smell. Maybe they should cut down on perfume and cologne, or stop reheating fish for lunch.
- It should be microwaved. Microwaving meals tend to emit fewer scents than other methods of cooking.

- Sniff the tasty thing. Surround yourself with smells that make you feel good. Mint, lemon, ginger, and cinnamon are more likely to relieve nausea than aggravate it.
- Keep your nose busy. Chew on some gum or chew on some hard candy to distract yourself from the scents. Peppermint sweets, in particular, may aid alleviate nausea.
- Go ice cold. Because your perceptions of taste and smell are so closely linked, eating cold versions of your favorite meals may assist. A cold steak sandwich or salmon salad may appeal to your stronger nose more than grilled steak or salmon, which may taste and smell better when served hot.

Can I avoid having a heightened sense of smell when pregnant?

Unfortunately, there is no way to educate your nose to be less sensitive while your hormones are high. This is one of those mom-to-be moments you'll have to put off until later in the pregnancy (or after your baby is born).

I wasn't sensitive to odors at home throughout my pregnancy. But smelling the cleaning solutions, air fresheners, and antiseptic soaps throughout the hospital made me sick. To combat the nausea-inducing odors, I kept a bottle of eucalyptus ointment in my pocket and rubbed a little under my nose as needed. The scent masked out the bad smells surrounding me, alleviated my nausea, and was comforting. Dr.

Rallie McAllister, a Lexington, Kentucky, mother of three kids and co-author of "The Mommy MD Guide to Pregnancy and Birth,"

Chapter 4: Tips to Combating Fatigue during Pregnancy

Here are some effective techniques to combat pregnancy exhaustion.

1. Maintain a Healthy Diet

To combat pregnant weariness, Dr. Weil recommends eating a fulfilling and healthy anti-inflammatory diet. Consume a variety of organic fruits and vegetables and limit your intake of processed meals. You should also avoid carbs that digest quickly, such as white bread, since they lead you to "crash" and feel tired. Eating a low-fat, high-iron, high-protein diet (if you can tolerate it) may also assist. Also, remain hydrated and take your prenatal vitamin during your pregnancy—and for at least six months afterward.

2. Daily Physical Activity

Commit to daily exercise, even if you are exhausted. Aerobic activity, such as brisk walking, according to Dr. Weil, nearly always helps you feel better. Exercise also helps you sleep better and enhances your mood by generating endorphins.

3. Get Enough Rest

Accept your need for additional sleep by going to bed at a time that allows you to sleep for eight to nine hours. Dr. Weil recommends taking catnaps every 15 to 20 minutes to recharge your batteries. Oversleeping, on the other hand, might make you feel even wearier.

4. Caffeine should be limited.

According to the American College of Obstetricians and Gynecologists, moderate caffeine consumption (less than 200 milligrams or 112 cups of coffee per day) does not increase the risk of miscarriage or preterm birth. Despite this, Dr. Weil does not recommend drinking caffeinated beverages or using natural stimulants such as Rhodiola (Rhodiola Rosea), eleuthero (Eleutherococcus senticosus), or ginseng during pregnancy. Their stimulant effects may impair your sleep and mood.

5. Relax

Pregnancy is hard on both your body and mind. You're making more blood, your heart rate is increasing, and you're consuming more water and nutrients. There's also the flood of emotions coursing through your mind, which can overwhelm you. Take advantage of the time to unwind before a wailing infant keeps you up all night. It is totally OK to change your schedule and cancel arrangements on occasion.

If you're pregnant and feeling chronic exhaustion, see your doctor; he or she may want to do testing to ensure you don't have anemia or hypothyroidism.

During my third pregnancy, I was in my final year of medical residency. Standing on my feet was exhausting, so I made extensive use of the rolling stools at our practice. Instead of walking, I'd roll it down the hall between exam rooms. I'd occasionally request that others push!

When you're tired, don't walk if you can stand, sit if you can stand, lie down if you can sit, and sleep whenever you can. Dr. Rallie McAllister, a Lexington, Kentucky, mother of three kids and co-author of "The Mommy MD Guide to Pregnancy and Birth,"

5. Preparing Pets for the Newborn

Your pets are probably already on to you. Your animals will most likely become aware of what's going on as your pregnancy progresses. After all, they're also parents. That's not to say they won't be jealous, especially if they've been your "babies" up until now. Try the following ways to protect your dogs, cats, or other creatures from being too nervous when the baby arrives:

- Make a racket

Babies make a variety of new noises. Turning on your baby swing or toys that create sounds (or even playing recordings of newborns crying) might help your pets adjust to the new soundtrack in your house.

- Introduce odors

Allow them to smell the new items you're purchasing for the baby (diapers, lotions, powders) to get acclimated to the new fragrances.

- Make new rules.

Begin preparing them for any new rules, such as changes to when and where they are permitted in the house.

- Ignore them sometimes.

Because you'll be spending considerably less time pampering your dogs after the baby arrives, you may help them adapt by gradually reducing your time with them now. It may be tempting to get in as much snuggle time as possible before the baby arrives (we know it's difficult!), but the gradual adjustment is considerably easier for an animal than abruptly terminating them when you bring home your new babe. Your spouse may also assist by developing a stronger bond with the pets and redistributing some of the attention rather than taking it away.

- Bring in the infants.

Inviting friends to bring their new children over may help your pets adjust to having a baby around, as well as enable you to see how your pets respond to kids. Make sure to keep an eye on them!

- Stop harmful behaviors right now.

Train your pets not to jump on the crib, jump in your lap without your permission (that's where the baby will be!), or engage in potentially dangerous behaviors such as jumping, swatting, or nibbling. Some mothers use aluminum foil or double-sided tape to train their cats not to jump on the crib and changing table (both materials tend to freak felines out).

- Visit the veterinarian.

Don't forget to have your pets checked out by a veterinarian before the baby arrives to ensure they're healthy and up to date on vaccinations. Remember to plan for your pets' care while you're away delivering that baby!

Finally, take a deep breath and trust that everything will be fine. It may take some getting used to, but everyone will adjust to the new family member in no time.

"Our cat was our baby before we had children. Because the cat was already five years old when our daughter was born, we were concerned about how she would react to the baby. We were correct. The cat was not pleased when the baby arrived! Fortunately, we had purchased a crib tent to keep the cat out. Dr. Mary Mason, a St. Louis physician and mother of two boys."

6. **Back Pain Treatment**

Back discomfort is a frequent complaint during pregnancy, and it's not surprising. You're gaining weight, your center of gravity shifts, and your hormones loosen the ligaments in your pelvic joints. However, you may often avoid or alleviate back discomfort during pregnancy.

Chapter 5:
Seven Methods For Getting Rid Of Pregnant Back Discomfort

1. Maintain proper posture.

Your center of gravity slips forward as your baby develops. You may compensate for falling forward by leaning back, which may strain the muscles in your lower back and lead to back discomfort during pregnancy. Keep the following posture principles in mind:

- Stand tall and straight.
- Keep your chest up.
- Maintain a comfortable posture with your shoulders back.

- Keep your knees loose.

For the best support, stand with a comfortably wide stance. If you must stand for extended amounts of time, place one foot on a low-step stool and take regular rests.

Good posture also entails sitting with caution. Select a chair with back support, or place a small pillow behind your lower back.

2. Purchase the necessary equipment.

Wear low-heeled (rather than flat) shoes with good arch support. Avoid high heels, which can further shift your balance forward and cause you to fall.

You might also consider wearing a maternity support belt. Although research on the effectiveness of maternity support belts is limited, some women find the additional support helpful.

3. Lift properly

When lifting a small object, squat down and lift with your legs. Don't bend at the waist or lift with your back. It's also important to know your limits. Ask for help if you need it.

4. Sleep on your side

Sleep on your side, not your back. Keep one or both knees bent. Consider using pregnancy or support pillows between your bent knees, under your abdomen, and behind your back.

5. Try heat, cold, or massage

While evidence to support their effectiveness is limited, massage or the application of a heating pad or ice pack to your back might help.

6. Include physical activity in your daily routine

Regular physical activity can keep your back strong and might relieve back pain during pregnancy. With your health care provider's OK, try gentle activities — such as walking or water exercise. A physical therapist also can show you stretches and exercises that might help.

You might also stretch your lower back. Rest on your hands and knees with your head in line with your back. Pull in your stomach, rounding your back slightly. Hold for several seconds, then relax your stomach and back — keeping your back as flat as possible. Gradually work up to 10 repetitions. Inquire with your doctor about different stretching activities.

7. Consider alternative therapy.

Acupuncture may help with back discomfort during pregnancy, according to some studies. Chiropractic care may also be beneficial to certain ladies. However, further study is required. If you're thinking about trying an alternative treatment, talk to your doctor first. Make it a point to inform the chiropractor or acupuncturist that you are pregnant.

When should you visit your healthcare provider?

Consult your healthcare provider if you have severe back pain during pregnancy or back pain that lasts more than two weeks. He or she may advise you to take acetaminophen (Tylenol, for example) or to seek other treatment.

Keep in mind that back pain during pregnancy might be a sign of preterm labor or a urinary tract infection. If you have back pain during pregnancy that's accompanied by vaginal bleeding, fever, or burning during urination, contact your healthcare provider right away.

"Late in one pregnancy, I had sciatica - pain in the lower back that runs down the leg. There's not much you can do about that when you're pregnant. I got a massage from a massage therapist who specialized in treating pregnant women. It helped temporarily. Better yet was the hour of relaxing and being pampered. Dr. Lezli Braswell is a mother of a daughter and two sons

and a family medicine physician in Columbus, Ga."

7. Breathing Easy

First of all, try not to worry too much about shortness of breath during pregnancy. Although you may feel as if you're getting less air, high levels of progesterone help you take deeper breaths to get enough oxygen into your blood. And because your blood volume is higher during pregnancy, more oxygen passes back and forth across the placenta as you inhale and exhale, says Dr. Riley.

You can relieve symptoms by giving yourself and your lungs as much breathing room as possible. Try adjusting your body position. Stand up straight, sit up tall, and sleep propped up on pillows to expand the space in your abdominal cavity. When you feel breathless, slow down—rushing makes your heart and lungs work harder. You can also consciously breathe in a way that raises your rib cage: Check that your ribs push out against your hands as you inhale deeply.

When to See a Doctor

If you are experiencing shortness of breath, be sure to mention this and any other symptoms you have to your healthcare provider during your prenatal visits. Also, if you are concerned at all, call them right away—what that's they're there for! Your doctor or midwife will be able to rule out or treat any underlying causes.

If you experience shortness of breath that's sudden, severe, or associated with chest pain or a faster pulse, get medical help immediately. A blood clot could have settled in your lungs, says Dr. Riley. This situation (called a pulmonary embolism) is a rare but dangerous occurrence among pregnant people, especially those with blood clots in their legs.

Be aware, too, that breathing problems can be caused by pneumonia. Usually accompanied by fever, chest discomfort, and cough, pneumonia is the third-leading cause of mortality among pregnant adults, says Dr. Riley. Pneumonia may be viral or bacterial, and with either kind, possible problems might include respiratory failure, early delivery, or infections that can be deadly for you and your baby.

What to Do If You Go Into Labor Early

You should also seek medical advice if you have asthma that worsens during pregnancy. Many asthma medicines are considered safe while expecting. During pregnancy, doctors normally prefer to provide inhaled asthma drugs since they have a more localized impact and perform effectively. However, if your chest feels tight or your medication isn't working, see your doctor.

Furthermore, in rare situations, shortness of breath during pregnancy may be an indication of an underlying disease such as a heart ailment or cancer. Contact your doctor if your shortness of breath is more than merely annoying, does not improve when you change positions, or is accompanied by other worrying symptoms such as discomfort. They will be able to tell whether there is anything unusual going on other than the usual pregnancy-related shortness of breath.

Shortness of breath is fairly frequent during pregnancy and, in most situations, is not an indication of a health problem. It may still be bothersome and should be discussed with your doctor. Slowing down, changing positions, and relaxing as much as possible are the greatest strategies to get relief. And trust that, even if you don't feel like you're getting enough oxygen, your baby is getting it.

"Pregnant women may experience shortness of breath. My middle child was a long baby who I carried high in my ribs. I was so out of breath near the end that I thought the wind had been

knocked out of me. I tried to walk as much as possible rather than run, and I sat down frequently to catch my breath. Dr. Marra Francia, ob-gyn and mother of three girls in The Woodlands, Texas"

8. Managing Labor Pain

Pain During Labor and Delivery

Contraction of the uterine muscles and pressure on the cervix induce pain during childbirth. This pain manifests as severe cramping in the belly, groin, and back, as well as an aching sensation. Some women also have discomfort in their sides or thighs.

Other reasons for discomfort during labor include the baby's head pressing on the bladder and intestines and the delivery canal and vagina stretching.

Every woman has varied levels of pain during childbirth. It varies greatly across women and even between pregnancies.

The fact that the contractions keep coming — and that as labor advances, there is less and less time between contractions to relax — is typically what women find the most difficult.

Making Preparations

Here are some things you may start doing before or throughout your pregnancy to aid with labor pain:

Regular and moderate exercise (as prescribed by your doctor) will help strengthen your muscles and prepare your body for the stress of delivery. Exercise may also improve your endurance, which will be useful if you have a lengthy labor. The most essential thing to remember while exercising is not to overdo it - particularly if you're pregnant. Discuss with your doctor what he or she deems a safe workout regimen for you.

If you and your spouse take birthing courses, you'll learn various pain-management strategies, such as visualization and exercises meant to strengthen the muscles that support your uterus. The Lamaze technique and the Bradley method are the two most prominent delivery philosophies in the United States.

In the United States, the Lamaze technique is the most often employed approach. According to the Lamaze concept, birth is a normal, natural, and healthy procedure that women should be enabled to approach with confidence. Lamaze classes teach women how to reduce their perception of pain by using relaxation techniques, breathing exercises, distraction, or massage from a supportive coach. Lamaze has a neutral stance on pain medication, advising women to make an educated choice about whether it is appropriate for them.

The Bradley method (also known as Husband-Coached Birth) emphasizes a natural approach to birth and the baby's father's active participation as a birth coach. One major goal of this method is to avoid using medications unless absolutely necessary. The Bradley method also emphasizes good nutrition and exercise during pregnancy, as well as relaxation and deep-breathing techniques to help with labor. Although the Bradley method supports a medicine-free delivery experience, the lectures do explore unanticipated difficulties or scenarios, such as emergency cesarean sections.

Medicine-free approaches to alleviate discomfort during delivery include

- hypnosis
- yoga
- meditation
- walking
- counterpressure or massage
- shifting positions
- bathing or showering
- music listening

- distracting yourself by counting or performing an activity that keeps your mind otherwise occupied
- Pain relievers

A variety of pain medicines can be used during labor and delivery, depending on the situation. Many women rely on such medications, and it can be a huge relief when the pain is quickly relieved and all of one's energy is focused on getting through the contractions. Discuss the risks and benefits of each type of medication with your healthcare provider.

Analgesics. Analgesics alleviate pain but do not totally eliminate it. They have no effect on sensation or muscular action. They may be provided in a variety of ways. They may influence the whole body if administered intravenously (through an IV into a vein) or by injection into a muscle. These medications have the potential to induce sleepiness and nausea in the mother. They may also have an impact on the baby.

Regional anesthesia. When most women contemplate pain medication during childbirth, this is what they envision. These treatments may be utilized for pain reduction in both vaginal and cesarean section births by inhibiting sensation in certain body areas.

During labor and delivery, epidurals, a local anesthetic, remove the majority of discomfort from the whole body below the belly button, including the vaginal walls. An epidural includes an anesthesiologist administering medication via a tiny, tube-like catheter put in the woman's lower back. The dosage of medication may be adjusted to meet the demands of the individual lady. Because very little drug reaches the infant, this technique of pain alleviation typically has little impact on the newborn.

Epidurals do have certain downsides, including lowering a woman's blood pressure and making it harder to urinate. They may also give the mother irritation, nausea, and headaches. The hazards to the infant are limited, but they include complications induced by the mother's low blood pressure.

Tranquilizers. These medications do not treat pain, but they may assist to calm and relax nervous ladies. They are sometimes used in conjunction with analgesics. These medications, which may harm both the mother and the baby, are seldom utilized. They may also make it difficult for women to recall the events of their delivery. Consult your doctor about the dangers of tranquilizers.

Childbirth Without Induction

Some women want to give birth without taking any medication, instead relying on relaxation methods and regulated breathing to manage discomfort. Discuss this with your healthcare practitioner if you want to give birth without pain medication.

Things to Think About

considering the following when contemplating pain control during labor:

Medicines may alleviate some of your pain, but they are unlikely to alleviate all of it.

Labor may be more painful than you anticipated. When they're in labor, some women who claimed they didn't want any pain medication change their minds.

Some medications might cause your infant to become sleepy or cause changes in heart rhythm.

Consultation with Your Health Care Provider

You should discuss your pain management choices with the person who will deliver your baby. Learn what is available, how successful they are likely to be, and why it is preferable not to take certain medications.

If you wish to employ pain-relieving treatments other than medication, inform your healthcare professional and hospital personnel. You might also consider developing a birth plan outlining your wishes.

Remember that many women make pain relief choices at the last minute, often for very excellent reasons. Your capacity to bear delivery pain has nothing to do with your value as a mother. You may be ready to pick what pain management method works best for you if you prepare and educate yourself.

"When you're on your back and hooked up to IVs and monitors, it's hard to have a natural delivery. It is not a good idea to lie down. Walking was my trick to getting through labor. I

walked till I couldn't go any farther, and then I walked some more.

I continued going until I felt the baby begin to emerge. I didn't want to give birth in the corridor, so I climbed into bed and began pushing. Dr. Hana R. Solomon, a pediatrician in Columbia, Missouri, is a mother of four."

8. **Resting Prior to Delivery**

"I slipped in a pedicure the afternoon before my water broke. That was my last pedicure in a long time, and I was relieved that I got it in just before the deadline. Dr. Ashley Roman is a clinical assistant professor of obstetrics and gynecology at New York University School of Medicine and the mother of two girls."

9. **Spreading the Word**

"My eldest daughter's pregnancy was discovered soon before we went out to supper to celebrate my husband's birthday. I concealed the ultrasound picture in my handbag in a frame labeled "Daddy and Me." "I believe you should open your final gift first," I told my husband when he asked whether I wanted wine."

He recognized it immediately away and ordered a martini. I ordered iced tea. Dr. Marra Francis, ob-gyn and mother of three girls in The Woodlands, Texas

10.Increasing Calcium Consumption

"I have lactose intolerance and have never been able to consume dairy products. And I'm a wuss when it comes to eating those massive calcium tablets. Luckily, I discovered liquid calcium at a health food shop. A couple of teaspoons each day provided all of the calcium I need while pregnant without bothering my stomach. Dr. Rallie McAllister, a Lexington, Kentucky, mother of three kids and co-author of "The Mommy MD Guide to Pregnancy and Birth,"

11. Relaxing with meditation

"Meditation is an important aspect of my life. My life is fairly hectic. Sitting quietly in meditation allows my brain to rinse itself out like laundry. The ability to sit quietly and learn to be an observer is a valuable talent to have

throughout pregnancy - and parenthood. It makes you more attentive to what your children say. Dr. Nancy Rappaport is a Harvard Medical School associate professor of psychiatry and the mother of two children and a boy."

12.Nursery Decorations

I painted a large image of my elder daughter and the twins clutching balloons on the nursery wall while I was pregnant with twins. While I was painting it, my daughter walked into the room. She bolted, yelling, "Daddy, Mommy's painting on the wall!" Dr. Susan Wilder, mother of three girls and a family physician in Scottsdale, Ariz.

13. Getting Rid of the Bean

I consume four cups of coffee every day. You may consume one or two cups of coffee per day while pregnant, so I created a pot with half decaf and half normal coffee throughout my pregnancy. I could still have four cups, but only two of them would be caffeinated. Dr. Gina Dado is a mother of two girls and an obstetrician in Scottsdale, Arizona.

14. Choosing a Pediatrician

It's a good idea to get medical referrals from friends. I was able to ask people who were both friends and doctors because many of my friends are doctors. It's a good idea to ask doctors for recommendations to other doctors. They understand how to evaluate the doctors' clinical skills in addition to their bedside manner.

If none of your friends are doctors, consider asking your doctors for recommendations on pediatricians. Dr. Ayala Laufer-Cahana, a pediatrician in Wynnewood, Pa., is a mother of three.

15. Taking Pictures of Your Stomach

Photographing my pregnant belly was my favorite part of my pregnancy. I was afraid to do it too soon, but at week 32, my husband and I wrote "32" in lipstick on my belly and took a photo, and then we did it every week after that.

After that, we began writing messages on my belly before taking photos. It was entertaining! Dr. Jennifer Gilbert, a twin mother and ob-gyn in Paoli, Pa.

16. Attending Prenatal Checkups

Despite the fact that I'm a doctor, I had a lot of questions for my obstetrician. I started jotting down my questions because I couldn't remember them during the excitement of my visits. After misplacing my list several times, I began writing my questions in my datebook. If my next appointment was on Nov. 1, I'd write my questions on the "Nov. 1" page. I could jot down my questions whenever they came to mind, and they were easy to find when I met with my doctor. Dr. Rallie McAllister, a Lexington, Kentucky, mother of three kids and co-author of "The Mommy MD Guide to Pregnancy and Birth,"

- ***Prenatal Vitamin Supplementation***

Vitamins are useless if you vomit them. If you are experiencing morning sickness and are unable to swallow your prenatal vitamins, chew a children's vitamin instead. One popular brand contains 400 micrograms of folic acid, which is what most experts recommend pregnant women get each day. Dr. Ashley Roman is a clinical assistant professor of obstetrics and gynecology at New York University School of Medicine and the mother of two girls.

17.Easing Heartburn

When I was pregnant with triplets, I had unrelenting heartburn. I found that eating ice cream and drinking milk helped. The ice cream (along with the medication my doctor prescribed) relieved my heartburn enough that it didn't wake me up. Of course, I was waking up for a zillion other reasons by then. Dr. Sadaf T. Bhutta is an assistant professor of pediatric radiology at Arkansas Children's Hospital in Little Rock and the mother of a daughter and a set of triplets.

18.Having Fun With Sex

Before and during my pregnancy, my husband and I had a healthy sex life. The morning my water broke, we had sex. Sex was pleasurable for both of us. It's a good idea to save up a lot of "credit," because you won't be able to have sex for a while after the baby is born. Dr. J.J. Levenstein is a pediatrician in private practice in Burbank, California.

19.Managing Constipation

During my first pregnancy, I was constipated. During my second pregnancy, my doctor advised me to take a prenatal vitamin that also includes a stool softener. I assumed it was beneficial, and I was certain of it one morning

when I neglected to take it. Instead, I took a standard vitamin, and I felt like I couldn't defecate all day. Dr. Sonia Ng, a doctor and mother of two kids in Princeton, N.J.

20.Preparing Your Birth Bag

I packed reading materials, baby clothing, and my Boppy nursing pillow to assist me nursing about a week before I went into labor. I also brought my computer since the hospital provided wireless Internet access. Because the infant slept a lot, I was able to use my computer. Dr. Amy J. Derick, a dermatologist in Barrington, Ill., is a mother of a boy.

- **Getting Rid of Your Fears**

Pregnancy is exhausting. This is certainly fantastic practice for parenthood, which is significantly more difficult.

I knew at some point throughout my pregnancy that I was doing my best and then faking the rest. I quit attempting to manipulate every variable. We're all stumbling along. I simply try to make the best decision I can. Dr. Ellen Kruger is a mother of two adolescents and an ob-gyn in New Orleans.

- **Relieving Foot Pain**

Take care of your feet or they will make you pay. During my pregnancy, my favorite shoes were the brown Hush Puppies loafers that I still wear now. My arches used to hurt

incessantly before I began wearing those shoes. They kept my dogs calm. Dr. Tyeese Gaines Reid, mother of one and an emergency medicine doctor at Yale New Haven Hospital in New Haven, Conn.

21.Entering Labor

My husband and I both terrified when I went into labor. He's a cardiologist, and he told me to breathe. "How do you know I need to breathe?" I inquired. "It's what they do in every movie," my spouse said. So we imitated what we saw on TV and in movies, and it worked perfectly. Dr. Diane Truong, a doctor in Burbank, California, and mother of two children.

- **The First Time You See Your Baby**

"I can't express how I felt when my children were born. It was as if I had died and there was a Heaven with the prophets and angels, and you could look at them and know that they were actual people. My baby's eyelashes and fingernails appeared incredible and vivid to me. It felt hard just to gaze at them."

The Perfect Guide for Expecting Mothers...Share a testimony

www.ingramcontent.com/pod-product-compliance
Lightning Source LLC
LaVergne TN
LVHW050321160826
845677LV00014B/3506

* 9 7 9 8 3 7 1 1 4 2 6 5 8 *